We Use
Honey

by Zachary Cohn

Editorial Offices: Glenview, Illinois • Parsippany, New Jersey • New York, New York
Sales Offices: Needham, Massachusetts • Duluth, Georgia • Glenview, Illinois
Coppell, Texas • Sacramento, California • Mesa, Arizona

ISBN: 0-328-13176-8

9 10 V010 14

Some people keep bees.

Bees do many jobs.

They make sweet honey in their hives.

We use honey in many ways.

We can eat honey.

It is sweet and good!

We can take honey on a picnic.

We can use honey to cook.

We can use it to make bread.

We can also use it to make cakes.

We can use honey when we are sick.

It may help us feel good.

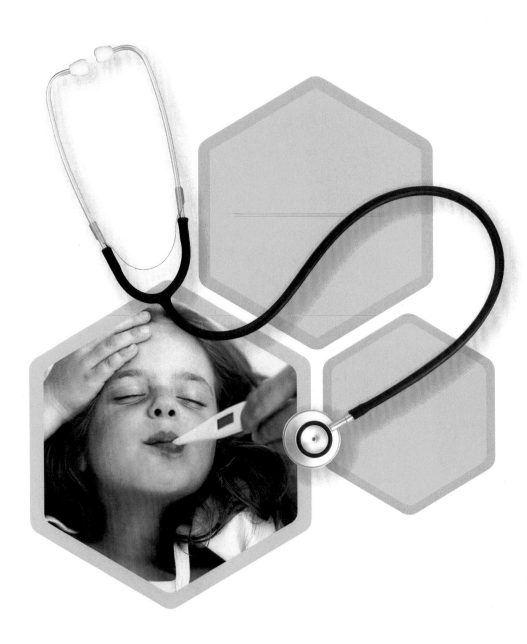

We can put honey in the tub.

We can mix honey with the water.

The honey can make our skin soft.

Bees make sweet honey.

We use it in many ways.

What are the ways your family uses honey?

Think of some other new ways to use it.

Think and Share

1. How is honey like sugar? How is honey different from sugar? Copy the chart and write your answers.

Honey	Sugar

2. What clues did the cover give you about this book?

3. Write the word *picnic* on your paper. Under each letter, write whether it is a vowel (v) or a consonant (c). How did this pattern help you read the word?

4. What do the pictures on pages 4 and 5 show you about honey?

Suggested levels for Guided Reading, DRA,™
Lexile,® and Reading Recovery™ are provided
in the Pearson Scott Foresman Leveling Guide.

Genre	Comprehension Skills and Strategy
Nonfiction	• Compare and Contrast • Draw Conclusions • Preview

Scott Foresman Reading Street 1.2.6

PEARSON

Scott
Foresman

scottforesman.com

ISBN 0-328-13176-8

90000

9 780328 131761

Lift Up Your VOICE

How to Be Mindful and Intentional For the Next Generation

ALMA L. CARR-JONES